A Journey Shared
Mateship, Malaya and Me

Stethoscope Publishing
105/2 Clarke St, Crows Nest, NSW 2065 Australia

First published in 2025 by Stethoscope Publishing

Text © John Meldrum
Cover artworks by Ted Lewis
Design by BKA+D

All rights reserved

Typeset in Adobe Garamont Pro

Printed and bound by Ingram Spark

978-1-7638987-5-2 (paperback)
978-1-7638987-6-9 (eBook)

A Journey Shared, Meldrum, John

 A catalogue record for this book is available from the National Library of Australia

A Journey Shared

Mateship, Malaya and Me

John Meldrum
with Sam Everingham

This book is dedicated to the memory of Barry Adams, a Malaya/Vietnam veteran, and Michael Vogt, a Vietnam veteran who passed away from Motor Neurone Disease in 2013. Any profits from book sales will be donated to the MND Foundation.

Annandale

Here I am, early 1962, in a truck heading to Kapooka., the Australian Army's mandatory basic training ground for all new soldier recruits. It's here, as a part of the 1st Recruit Training Battalion at Blamey Barracks near Wagga Wagga in southern NSW, that I'll spend twelve weeks learning the basics of Australian soldiering before moving on to specialised training.

These three short years will give me experiences I will never forget, shaping my values and life skills, and allowing me to ultimately become my own man. What I learn will underpin the achievements I go on to enjoy in my local community, in building a family and a career.

I was born on 26 January 1943, the third child in a working-class inner Sydney family. My father Fred was a storeman and occasional SP bookie, and my mother Elsie was a process worker in a Vulcanite rubber factory. They named me John Patrick. Mum went on to have two more boys. By the time my youngest sibling, Peter, was born, I was five years old, my eldest brother Bob was eight, my sister Judy was seven, and Len was just two. We all shared a tiny two-bedroom workers' terrace at 84 Taylor St, Annandale – pretty much a slum suburb. Our front door opened directly into my parents' bedroom. To reach our bedroom, we five children had to pass through their room. Understandably, there was no room for entertaining. But Dad used to run his SP bookie business from the front bedroom, using the metal grille window which faced onto the street as his 'business' counter.

84 Taylor St, Annandale

Primary school was at Annandale North. My dad drank to excess, so life at home could be difficult. I didn't like the way he drank, and our place was tiny, so I took to spending more time on the streets. To free up space in our cottage, my brother Bob moved in with my grandmother. As a teenager, Judy moved out to live with friends.

Often our folks had no clue where we were. I would run down to Glebe's Jubilee Oval to watch the older boys playing sport. Unusually for Sydney, as our local oval they played Aussie Rules. When I was nine I asked to join. We called ourselves the Balmain Magpies, modelling ourselves as the brother club to Collingwood in Melbourne. Later we rebranded as the Balmain Tigers, wore black jerseys with a yellow stripe, and became part of the Sydney AFL League. Aussie Rules became something of a passion.

By the 1950s, the competition had become more popular, with some matches attracting up to 5,000 spectators. However with no local schools offering the sport, there was a lack of junior players. I was often asked to play up in older age groups – under sixteens – then I'd back up and play under eighteens, and even reserve grade – at Jubilee Oval or across the canal at Federal Reserve. At Jubilee Oval there was a secret clubroom in the old viaducts which ran across the oval. We could drink and make all the noise we wanted, as no one could hear.

As the poor cousin of League and Union and facing increasing competition from Rugby League, in 1950, Aussie Rules switched its finals matches to Sundays. It also faced increasingly bad player behaviour, which it tried to quash through harsher suspensions.

To overcome my lack of funds in a home where we scrapped by, from an early age, I took on many odd jobs to earn money. Unfortunately I was never much of a saver, spending it much faster than I earned, sometimes on playing card games when I should have been at school.

One of the first income-producing ventures my friends and I came up with was to offer to look after cars parking in Annandale for the Trots. Harold Park Trots was a big deal in those days and Taylor Street was utilised by many to park their cars and walk across the bridge over the canal to the track.

As soon as a car parked, my friends and I, looking very official sporting a white coat and torch, would ask –'Sir, would you like us to look after your car till you return?'

Often the punters agreed and of course we would go elsewhere till the trots were over, but then rush back with our coat and torches, hoping they had a good win. It was a nice money-earner some of the time, but rest assured mostly not.

I also worked with the local milkman for a while. In those days milk was delivered to each household - in earlier days the milkman drove a horse and cart - and later a small truck.

Each household would leave out their empty milk bottles with cash for a replacement on their verandas. Imagine leaving money on your doorstep these days? It sure as eggs would not be there next morning.

Then I found work as a paperboy some mornings and afternoons. In the absence of television or the internet, people relied on either the radio or the morning and afternoon editions of the papers for news. It meant walking the streets delivering papers or jumping on the trams to sell papers – yelling out 'TELE OR THE HERALD.'

There was no paper barrow and the papers were much thicker than today. Instead we had a leather strap slung over our shoulders, with papers held by the strap against your chest. For me, the major problem was being so scrawly and skinny. Carrying loads weighing more than I did was bloody hard work. We would edge along the tram's outside ledge with our satchels. One time I fell off the moving tram, landing on the bitumen, as my newspapers flew in all directions.

If walking the streets, I would count out a certain number of papers and the Newsagent would drop off more at certain areas, for me to collect as my supplies ran low. If I was on the trams and ran out of papers, it was straightforward to take the tram back to the Newsagent to pick up more. The worst days were Thursdays and Sundays, given the editions those days were so thick.

Another job I found was working in the local Royal Theatre, selling snacks prior to the start of the movie and during the interval. I was sometimes behind the counter and other times walking down the aisles, yelling out 'Chocs. Peter Ice!'.

It was these jobs which enabled me to treat myself to a few little luxuries that my parents could never afford.

I progressed to Enmore Boys High but we all left school as soon as we could, after the Intermediate Certificate. When it was my turn to leave school it was 1958, I had failed the exams, was just fifteen years old, with little idea what I wanted to do. But I yearned to work.

I quickly found a role as a clerk processing salaries for AW Edwards – a building and construction business just a block or two from home. Very convenient, but tedious, boring work.

So my father instead arranged a job in the warehouse of an engineering company. After a few months, I was again promoted to accounts as a clerk. But, still a teenager, I was restless and bored, so now sixteen, I joined the local Army Reserve to while away my spare time. Meanwhile I found a position on the mail desk with United Artists Australasia – the local distributor of Hollywood films. The company distributed films worldwide for producers and directors not associated with major studios. Again I was promoted to a clerical role as assistant accountant. Here I had responsibility for recording each film's sales and deducting costs to calculate total revenue for each film, and then allocating what share we owed to each film's producer.

On the floor above, one of the major American studios – Warner Bros – had their Australian office. It boasted a small theatre where, every Friday, we sat down to enjoy a first release movie. I loved it.

United Artists was a good employer, my colleagues were friendly and looked out for me like family. Marcia, the receptionist, and Jan, in charge of electronic data processing, insisted on mothering me. Jan looked after the enormous mainframe computer which housed all the company's business records. It was so big it needed its own room. My boss, Joe Scicia, the firm's accountant, and another accountant, Tom, were early mentors. Though our administration manager, Paul Herbert, was not my favourite person, the company was, in hindsight, a great environment, giving me the chance to widen my social networks.

Every Friday many of the staff routinely had lunch together at the nearby Hyde Park Hotel. After one of these lunches, Herbert suggested that the junior staff return to work, while the senior management stay on to enjoy the afternoon. Affronted by what

I felt was an injustice, I walked out in a rage, telling Herbert he could stick my job. I resigned that day.

I later realised how childish my actions had been. If I had a little more life experience, I would not have stormed out. But the deed was done. I was nearly nineteen and needed an alternative.

I was still enjoying the Army Reserve, so I thought, why not give the regular Army a crack? It would provide an opportunity to escape Dad and our cramped living arrangements.

The Army offered various minimum periods of service – three, six or nine years. At my age, three years did not feel such a long commitment. If the career suited, I might continue – otherwise I could arrange a discharge.

The Army looked to offer a major adventure. Until now, the furthest I had ventured from Sydney's inner west was 120 kilometres north to Budgewoi on the Central Coast. Army service would give me the chance to see other parts of Australia – perhaps even other cultures.

So in November 1961, I completed the paperwork and presented my eight stone of skin and bones (categorised as 'slight') for the required medical examination. There was a dental exam to do, a chest x-ray and a long medical questionnaire. There was little to report. I was tall enough, at five feet and nine inches. Good eyesight, normal hearing, a bit of acne, normal blood pressure, my tonsils had been removed two months earlier, and an appendix scar from its removal five years earlier. But I was a heavy smoker. Despite the smoking, I was passed as fit for service. I was given my first tetanus inoculation. Life would never be the same again.

Learning The Ropes

I was shipped to Kapooka outside Wagga Wagga for my initial twelve weeks training. On arrival, I was confronted by rows of ageing Nissan huts – with only fans to battle the stifling summer heat. I felt like I had stepped back in time. I could picture Australia's Second World War volunteers – teenagers like me – shuffling in for their first taste of army training two decades earlier. I could sense the ghosts of their presence.

Until now, I had never used a broom in my life, never washed clothes or been up close with the Australian bush – let alone slept in a tent. Just weeks earlier I had been used to making my own choices about when I left my bed, when I ate and what I did in my spare time. But here everything ran to a schedule based on daily orders. It was like being back at school, with far more discipline. Everyone I came across was very down-to-earth. There were no pretensions. If a bloke was being a wanker, he'd be told to his face.

These first three months introduced us to rifles, grenades, marching drills, keeping equipment presentable, and getting used to obeying orders without question. This last responsibility required some mental recalibration in my rebellious head. Despite the heat and discipline, I enjoyed the training and the spit and polish required.

An experience early in my time at Kapooka illustrates what army life could be like. There were huge differences in the personalities and, hence, the behaviour of the Non-Commissioned Officers (NCOs) who ruled our lives. The bad ones could be just intolerable.

One day in camp I dropped a cigarette. One particular NCO noticed and ordered an especially sadistic punishment. I was to traipse around the camp for days, collect every cigarette butt I could find and sew them together. While the NCO considered his punishment hilarious, I felt shamed. It was then I realised three years in the Service was going to be my limit. I would make the most of those years, but then I was out.

In fact most of the NCOs were far more reasonable in their approach to us grunts and I learned a lot at Kapooka. Life in camp was companionable, what with mess hall dinners together each night and a club where you could enjoy a few beers.

Forced to interact, I rapidly made friends with characters from various backgrounds: Barry Adams from Albury; Ken Mcleod, who had grown up in inner Sydney also; Brian McGrath, a Victorian and, like me, a VFL player; along with another Victorian (and VFL player), a guy we nicknamed Bing Crosby, who had one of the biggest egos. A few Queenslanders also became mates – Dutchy Holland, much older, a drover who had an enormous capacity for drink.

Arms training at Kapooka with mates

Horsing around

Me (right) horsing around with Beetle with Kapooka Nissan huts in background

A lovely sincere Spaniard was also part of our group. Cisco had arrived in Australia with a university degree which the Australian authorities refused to accept. So had joined the Army, throwing in his fortune with us misfits.

Napoleon at Kapooka

Then there was Ray Logue from Cairns – one of the few married recruits. We were jealous to learn that Ray was allowed regular leave for conjugal visits to see his wife who had rented a flat in nearby Wagga Wagga. In contrast, we were allowed just one weekend in Wagga during our three months of training. The event felt a little like being released from jail.

But as long as we were not too rowdy, the Wagga locals welcomed our patronage – we brought money into the town's economy. We VFL fans had a lot to talk about – what team did they follow? Would the planned purpose-built mega-stadium, VFL Park, really hold 155,000 fans? Would Sydney Naval again win this year's NSW premiership? I made Brian and Bing promise to join my beloved Balmain Tigers when we were back in Sydney.

It was drummed into us that our actions could affect so many. One bad apple could have a roll-on effect at platoon up to battalion level. So I was quick to learn that even if I failed to gel with someone, I had work with them. Fortunately, I worked with most recruits without serious problems. But with some, you could feel the dissention between them.

Once I adapted to the army routine, most of it was enjoyable. I was picking up skills that civilian life would never expose me to – learning how to shoot, survival in the bush, relying on one's own abilities, and protecting mates without the oversight of family. We needed to work as a team.

Within those twelve weeks as well as my basic army training I picked up some invaluable life lessons. I felt a little more mature.

I remember one Army recruit at the grenade range. Given the signal to put his training to use – withdraw the pin and lob a live hand grenade – he panicked. After pulling the pin, he dropped the grenade like a stone. We all stared in disbelief, before scrambling to shelter behind a nearby protective wall. The grenade exploded with a deafening boom. Our platoon had escaped being maimed or killed with milliseconds to spare. As what-ifs looped continuously in my mind, I found little sleep that night.

At the end of our three months basic training, we had to sit exams in English, maths and social studies, then make a decision around more specialised training – infantry, service or artillery ? The majority of my new mates and I chose infantry – the old foot soldier.

On 12 April 1962 I was posted to Ingleburn on the outskirts of Sydney, for specialised infantry training. Infantry required a higher level of fitness than other groups, so it was here that my

physical training escalated. Training included proper infantry training, map reading, weapons training, teamwork, spit and polish, bush work, and parade drills.

Artillery range training with the M62 machine gun

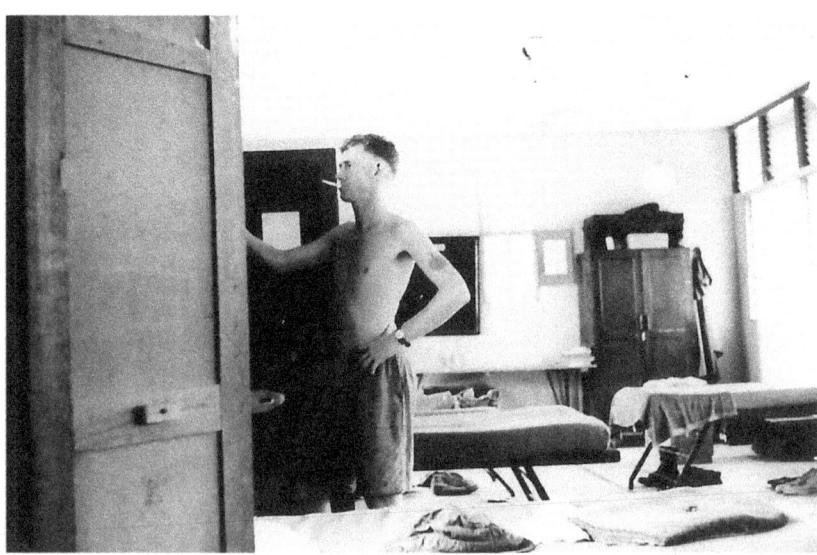

My 8-bed dorm at Ingleburn - smoking allowed, but no aircon

Our accommodation was a slight step up from Kapooka. The huts at Ingleburn were likely built during the Korean War in the early 1950s. Here, we were not camp-bound. If you lived in Sydney, you could go home on weekends. Liverpool, a much bigger suburb, was close to Ingleburn and the roads were quieter then. Driving home to Annandale was reasonably quick. It meant I could continue my footy with Balmain.

For the country recruits, many had never seen a big city. So weekend outings were highly anticipated, involving seeing the sights – beaches, Harbour Bridge, the Rocks as well as pub nights.

I was fairly fit, enjoying life, and the NCOs and officers treated us more like adults. I bought a cheap Holden FX to allow me to travel home on weekends. It meant I could catch up with old friends from my own neighbourhood.

My first car, a Holden FX

Life was good. I was enjoying infantry training plus new army friends. I also joined the footy team at the Ingleburn base. My army mate Bing, who I'd convinced to play for Balmain, would yell on the field: 'Give me the ball'. He was sure he could score. I wish that had been true.

A new guy arrived at Ingleburn from the Signal Corp. McKenzie was a giant – well over six foot, and built like a brick shithouse, a lovely bloke sober. But once inebriated, he was a bloody nuisance. He had got into trouble with alcohol in the Signal Corp which had led to his transfer to infantry, unsure of his future.

I recall my first forced march of about 42 kilometres at Ingleburn – fully dressed, with a heavy pack, plus weapons. The terrain included interminable hill climbs – a mandatory part of training. About halfway through the course, I was struggling. Along beside me suddenly appeared Private McKenzie. Grabbing my pack and rifle he looked me in the eye.

'You are going to finish this march by hook or by crook.'

McKenzie ploughed on, shouldering two packs and two weapons. Even without a load, I struggled to keep up. But I made it.

My remaining time at Ingleburn was not really taxing. I remember the Recreation Club was named Chown Club, after a VC winner. Co-incidentally, my mother's maiden name was Chown.

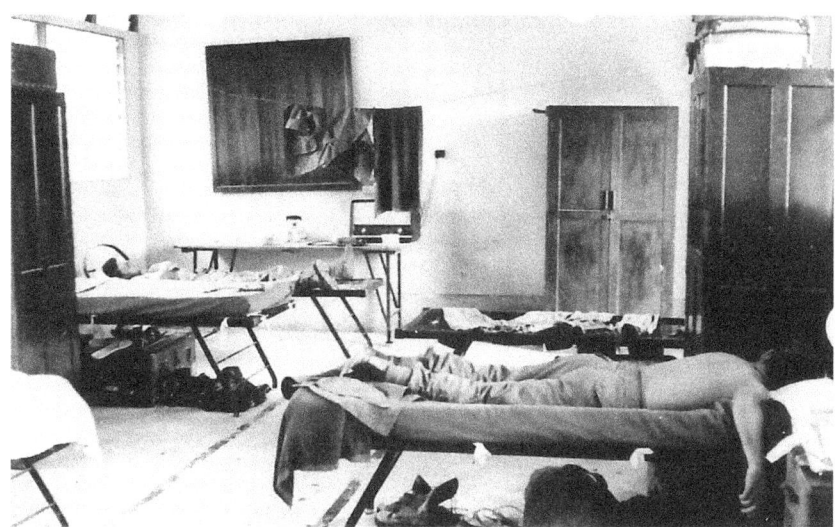
Relaxing in the Ingleburn dorm

*

We were advised our training was complete. Our group of around forty newly trained privates were being posted to Malaya to join 2 RAR (Second Battalion, Royal Australian Regiment). We were to report to South Head transit camp for air transfers in two weeks.

Malaya? None of us even knew where the place was.

For the next two weeks, with all that time to ourselves, we were in limbo. A lot of the fellows were big drinkers. Given most were from interstate or the country, every night became a booze up. Dutchy Holland fell asleep with a cigarette in his hand and nearly burnt the hut down. McKenzie drank non-stop. One day, McKenzie and some mates were accosted by some NCOs while walking across the rifle range with a few bottles of wine. McKenzie stuffed a bottle under his shirt.

'Private, what is under your shirt?' one NCO challenged him.

'A deformed left rib, SIR!'

I think only the fact that we were about to be posted offshore prevented an insubordination charge. Instead the NCO shrugged, pleading with the blokes to behave themselves.

There were a few other minor incidents, so I was lucky to be able to escape back home at times.

*

As we clambered aboard transports bound for the South Head transit barracks in Watsons Bay, all our NCOs and officers lined up at the Ingleburn gates, joshing with us about a safe trip and not to bother returning. Twelve days earlier we had started a course of injections to vaccinate us against cholera. We were advised boosters would be needed every six months, given where we were headed.

But once at South Head, it turned out they were not ready for us. So we were trucked back to Ingleburn. Their Ingleburn trainers groaned as the trucks returned through the gates, realising they were not yet rid of their young charges. Fortunately it was only for a couple of days.

*

On 19 August 1962 our platoon finally departed – in full uniform – on a Qantas commercial flight. Working class Australians simply did not travel internationally in the 1960s and even amongst the middle classes, few could afford air travel. Indeed most of us had never boarded a plane. So the excitement and anticipation of a government-funded overseas deployment were high.

The aircraft seemed huge. With still no concept of why we were being deployed to Malaya, we found ourselves refuelling in Darwin before the next leg to Djakarta, Indonesia. At the time, amidst fears of a military threat from our closest Asian neighbour, Indonesia and Australia were not on friendly terms.

In Djakarta, armed soldiers escorted us from the plane to a cramped room in the terminal, where we were held until the plane was ready for us to re-board.

On 21 August we arrived at Kuala Lumbar airport, then onto a truck to our new home, Camp Terendak – thirteen miles north of Malacca on the Malacca–Masjid Tanah Road – an enormous military battalion for which full construction and occupation had just been completed. It would be my first day as a private with 2 RAR.

Malaya — A Cultural Melting Pot

Malaya still housed communist insurgents, so we had been posted, along with battalions of British and New Zealand troops in an effort to combat these. Originally known as Fort George before being renamed Terendak Garrison – after Terendak Hill on which the camp is located – the site belonged to the British Commonwealth. It took in close to 1,500 acres, with an additional training area of 3,500 acres, the largest of several Malaya-based camps.

Its construction had begun back in 1957, partially funded by the governments of the United Kingdom, Australia and New Zealand. It needed to house the 28th Commonwealth Infantry Brigade Group after their relocation from North Malaya.

In any location, a garrison had enough units to be self-sufficient – essentially a large military town. Terendak, like any garrison, contained a military hospital, transport unit, supply depot (for foodstuffs, fuel, oil and lubricants), education centre, civil labour unit, hygiene and malaria control unit, Army Depot Police Detachment and Barracks Services (for single men), an airstrip, married quarters, and shopping precinct. Terendak's southwestern border was the Strait of Malacca. It would not be fully completed until 1964. A combined forces Air Force unit was stationed further north at Penang.

The Pommies, led by Lieutenant-General Sir Roger Bower, were represented by the Kings' Own Yorkshire Light Infantry regiment – Koylies for short. The regiment had served all over the world, including Burma, India, Africa, Italy, France, Germany and Cyprus. First deployed to Malaya in 1948 to take part in peacekeeping and counter-insurgency operations during the Malayan Emergency, they had returned to Malaya at the same time we arrived.

As a lowly private, I understood none of this geo-political complexity at the time. It is important to pause here to provide some historical background to our deployment into this very complex cultural landscape.

Malaya had for centuries been exposed (or subjected) to cultural influences from surrounding powers. Between the 7th and 13th centuries many of the region's small, often prosperous, maritime trading states likely came under the loose control of a great Indianised empire based in Sumatra. At various times, other Indianised powers of Southeast Asia also claimed the region. These early cultural forces in Malaya influenced political ideas, social structures, rituals, language, arts, and other traditions.

From the 13th through the 17th century, Sunni Islam, carried chiefly by Arab and Indian merchants, spread widely through Southeast Asia. The religion's complex theology held much appeal for farmers and merchants in the coastal regions.

The Siamese came to control some of the northern Malay sultanates but these included many often-feuding chiefdoms, with wars within and between the sultanates erupting from time to time. From the Europeans' perspective, the sultanate system was politically unstable.

During the 17th century many Minangkabau people migrated from western Sumatra, bringing with them a matrilineal sociocultural system by which property and authority descended through the female line. The political pluralism of Malaya in the 18th century also facilitated large-scale penetration by Buginese people from southwestern Celebes. Immigrants from Java, Celebes and Sumatra assimilated into the existing Malay community over time.

Except for Malacca, Western influence was negligible until the late 18th century. The British sought a source for goods to be sold in China, and in 1786 the British East India Company acquired the island of Penang, off Malaya's northwest coast. The island soon became a major trading centre with a chiefly Chinese population. In 1819, British representative Stamford Raffles occupied Singapore as a strategic location at the southern end of the Strait of Malacca and a fine harbour as the centre for Britain's economic and political thrust. The British attracted Chinese immigrants, and soon the mainly Chinese port became the region's dominant city and a major base for Chinese economic activity in Southeast Asia.

Britain next obtained Malacca from the Dutch in 1824 and so governed the three major ports in the Strait of Malacca – Penang, Malacca, and Singapore – collectively called the Straits Settlements. With the opening in 1869 of the Suez Canal, the feuding Malay states were little prepared for the impact of increased European commercial activity, including the steady immigration of Chinese. By the early 19th century, the Chinese – driven to emigrate by increasing poverty and instability in China – began settling in large numbers in Malaya, where they cooperated with local Malay rulers to mine tin.

The Chinese organised themselves into tightly knit communities and formed alliances with competing Malay chiefs. Chinese settlers also established towns such as Kuala Lumpur. The Chinese and Malays increasingly became entrenched in an inadequately integrated sociopolitical structure that continually generated friction between the two communities.

British investors were attracted to Malaya's potential mineral wealth but were concerned about political unrest. As a result, by the 1870s local British officials began to intervene in internal affairs – establishing political influence through a system of British 'advisers'. Initial intervention was crude and incompetent; the first British resident to Perak was murdered by outraged Malays. Gradually, the British appointed more able representatives. By 1914 Britain had achieved control over nine sultanates, without interfering in matters of religion, customs or the symbolic political role of the sultans. The various states were increasingly integrated to form British Malaya.

The British administration eventually achieved peace and security. Their officials believed that traditional class divisions should be maintained. Their policies promoted the planting of pepper, gambier (a plant producing a resin for tanning and dyeing), tobacco, oil palm, and rubber, which along with tin became the region's major exports.

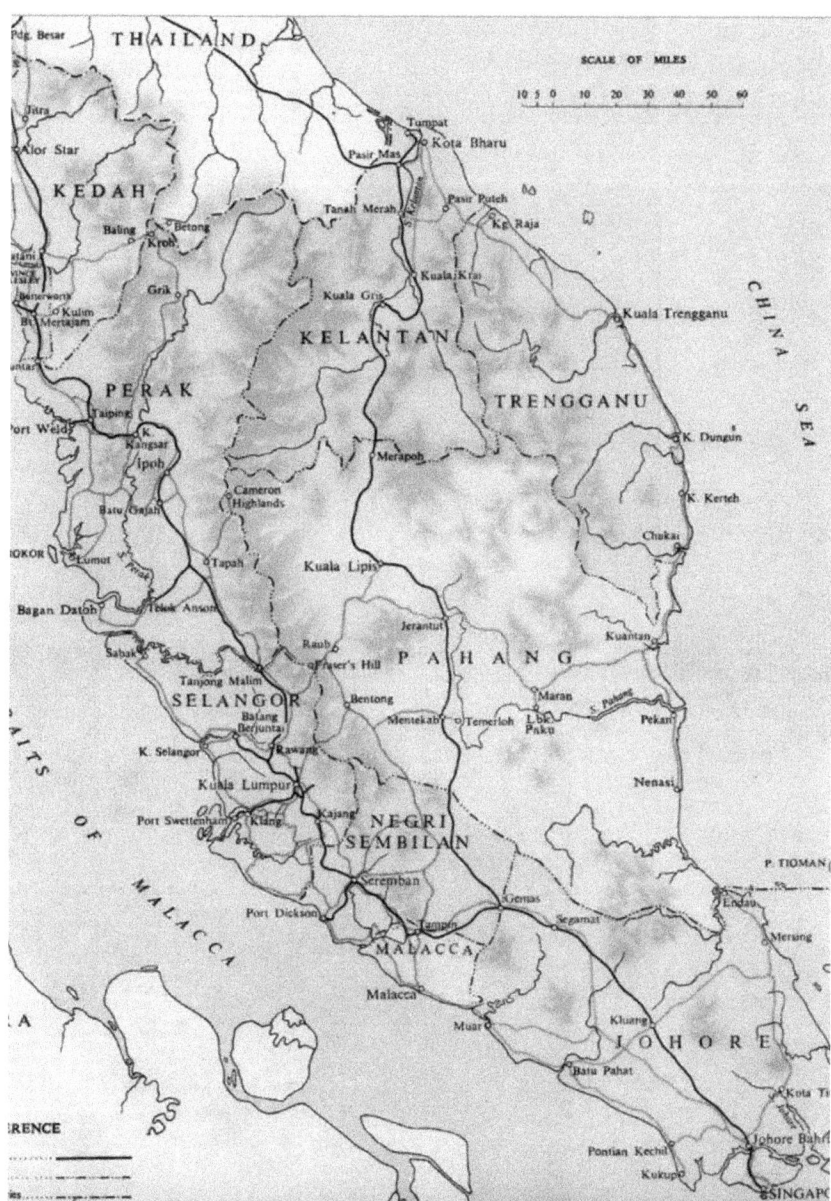

1955 Survey Department Map of Malay Peninsula

British authorities constructed railways and road networks linking the tin fields to the coast; port facilities also were improved. By the early 20th century thousands of acres of forest had been cleared

Kuala Lumpur street scene

Visiting Kuala Lumpur in 1962

for rubber plantations. Malaya would become the world's greatest exporter of natural rubber. The export played a crucial role in the economy, becoming a major source of revenue for Britian. Initially, small plots were planted, but by 1920 there were nearly one million acres of plantations. The industry was heavily reliant on British capital, with many plantations owned by European companies[1].

The British also improved public health facilities, reducing tropical diseases, and facilitated the building of government Malay schools and Christian mission schools; the Chinese generally had to develop their own schools. These separate systems helped reinforce the pluralistic society.

Between 1800 and 1941 several million Chinese entered Malaya as labourers, miners, planters and merchants. The Chinese eventually became part of a prosperous, urban middle class that controlled retail trade. South Indian Tamils were imported to work on rubber estates. Colonial authorities used 'divide and rule' tactics to maintain control. With most Malays in villages, Chinese in towns, and Indians on plantations, different ethnic groups kept to their own neighbourhoods, followed different occupations, practiced their own religions, spoke their own languages, operated their own schools, and later formed their own political organisations. But by the 1930s, ethnically oriented nationalist currents began to rise.

The occupation by Japan during World War II generated tremendous changes. Malaya's economy was disrupted, and communal tensions worsened because Malays and Chinese reacted differently to Japanese control. Pro-communist, predominantly Chinese guerrillas resisted. Increasing politicisation and conflict within and among ethnic groups developed as a result of economic hardship and selective repression; the Chinese and Malays realised

---

1 *Post-independence, rubber remains a significant agricultural commodity for Malayasia, with smallholder farmers now the main producers.*

that British domination was not everlasting. Nonetheless, most people welcomed the Japanese defeat in 1945.

After the end of the war, some local self-government was introduced. The British proposed a single Malayan Union, incorporating all the Malayan territories except Singapore, that would diminish state autonomy and give equal political and citizenship rights to non-Malays. But a tremendous upsurge against this plan in the form of strikes, demonstrations and boycotts resulted in the United Malays National Organisation (UMNO) being founded to progress Malay nationalism. Instead the British began to negotiate with UMNO about Malaya's future.

The negotiations resulted in the Federation of Malaya in 1948 which unified the territories but provided special guarantees of Malay rights, including the position of sultans. This alarmed the more radical and impoverished Chinese community. So the same year, the Communist Party of Malaya – a mostly Chinese movement – began a guerrilla insurgency to overthrow the colonial administration.

Britain had declared a State of Emergency in Malaya in June 1948. The Koylies arrived that year and Australian involvement began with the deployment of two Royal Australian Air Force Squadrons in 1950. But the violent struggle was supported by only a small part of the Chinese community.

The colonial powers forced many rural Chinese into tightly controlled new villages near or along the roadsides. Although this isolated villagers from guerrillas, it also increased the colonial government's unpopularity. The British addressed political and economic grievances as well as the insurgency, further isolating the rebels.

Finally, British officials started negotiations for independence with ethnic leaders. Tired of the ongoing problems, Britain wanted out. A Malayan, Chinese and Indian coalition contested national elections in 1955 and won all but one seat. This established a permanent pattern of a ruling coalition that united ethnically based parties, with UMNO as the major force.

From 1955, with unrest continuing, Australian Army and Royal Australian Navy personnel arrived. Each battalion took turns going out to the jungle for months at a time in efforts to drive out the communist insurgents. Over the next five years 39 Australian servicemen would give up their lives and 27 were wounded in the guerilla skirmishes.

Finally in August 1957, the Federation of Malaya achieved independence. The British retained some authority after that, but mainly in an assistance role. The arrangement favoured the Malays politically, with the kingship rotating among the Malay sultans, but the Chinese were granted liberal citizenship rights and maintained strong economic power. Kuala Lumpur became the federal capital. Singapore remained as a British crown colony.

However, communist disruption and hence anti-communist operations dragged on. Not until July 1960 did the Malayan government officially declare the emergency over. So why did Australian forces stay on?

It seems there were two key reasons. In 1961 a proposal by British officials emerged for a federated state to include Malaya, Sarawak, North Borneo, Brunei and Singapore. British leaders had proposed this as a way of terminating their now burdensome colonial rule over these dependencies, even though those states were historically and ethnically distinct from Malaya and each other. It was a marriage of convenience.

Most accepted the idea of merging with the new federation and when the Philippines claimed North Borneo, basing it on the Sultan of Sulu's historical sovereignty, support for the proposal increased. But Malaya's neighbour, Indonesia, was vehemently opposed to such a plan. The ongoing anti-communist sentiment amongst Westen nations was another complication. A breakdown in political, economic and social relations between Indonesia and Malaya ensued, leading to what would become known as the Indonesia–Malaysia or Borneo confrontation (*Konfrontasi* was the local name for the conflict).

Jungle Patrols

My new unit, 2 RAR, had previously spent two years in Malaya between 1955 and 1957, during the Malayan Emergency, losing 14 men in battles against the communists. It had joined the 28th Commonwealth Brigade again in October 1961. When I arrived in August 1962 we were committed to anti-communist operations, searching for the remnants of the Malayan National Liberation Army communists who had a nucleus of between 500 and 600 well-trained guerillas along the Thai–Malay border. While Malays in the main did not take to communism – happy with what they had – in contrast, the Malayan Communist Party were mainly Chinese with a small number of Malays.

It was our battalions of Australian, British and New Zealand servicemen, Gurkahs[2], Malayan Army and police, plus Australian air force troops who were here to hunt out those remnant forces.

---

2 For around 150 years Gurkha soldiers (Nepalis or Nepali-speaking Indian nationals) had been recruited for the Nepali, Indian and British Armies and for United Nations peacekeeping forces and war zones around the world.

*

As my first weekend in a foreign country approached, I was delighted to learn I had the weekend off. With mates I took a taxi the 145 kilometres to Kuala Lumpur, Malaya's capital. Taxis were an unheard-of luxury back in Sydney for a kid like me from a poor background. But each of us received a lump-sum overseas allowance on arrival, and taxis were cheap as chips, so long trips by taxi were common.

Kuala Lumpur – like most of the country – was defined by a mix of Malays, Chinese and Indians. Locals were very friendly. It was a very different city to Sydney. Different religions, different churches, with street markets chock-full of food vendors and other stall holders. Every day's experience was so different to life at home. For the Aussie country boys, the contrast must have been even more stark.

In Kuala Lumpur, we caroused in the many bars, and spent time getting to know the locals, picking up some of the language and history of the city. The first Malay phrases I learnt were 'Primai Kasai' (thank you) and 'Sama-sama' (you're welcome). The phrases stayed with me. Even today when I go out and come across a Malaysian serving in the store, I say 'Primai Kasai'. I receive some astonished looks at times.

Back in camp on the Monday, I was told I was being despatched to the jungle to join 1 Platoon, given they needed reinforcements. This was much earlier than I expected. I had only been in the country a week. Officially, we were supposed to be in camp a few weeks to acclimatise to both local and camp procedures before jungle deployment. Instructed to change into long trousers, I was assigned a small surprisingly heavy backpack – it had to fit a hammock, blow-up mattress, mosquito net and change of clothes.

I was escorted by Corporal Richardson, who was returning to 1 Platoon after a period in camp for medical treatment. The guy had tickets on himself as a guide, insisting he was the best scout in the Army. We would locate our platoon in under a few hours, he assured me.

But after hours of walking, the light began to fade. He admitted we were lost. We would have to camp here for the night. So we began puffing air into our canvas mattresses. The corporal then took out a pannikin of salt and commenced encircling each with a thin white border of the stuff.

'What is this for?' I asked.

'To stop the soldier ants,' he grunted back.

I said nothing, but thought, this guy is crazy. I was wrong.

During the night I awoke to a chomping sound. I opened my eyes wide and flicked on my torch only to see what appeared to be millions of soldier ants swarming toward us. But as they reached the salt barrier, their linear progress seemed to magically divert around our beds, before realigning their route to continue their forward advance. I was gobsmacked.

I had a newfound relief for my guide's company. Without his forethought, the ants may have chomped their way through us in their blind march. Admittedly it was my first night in the jungle, but I found it impossible to fall properly back to sleep, imagining a thousand ants gnawing through my ears, eyes, mouth and anus.

Next morning we packed up and resumed our trek. Our brilliant scout still had no clue where we were. About an hour on, coming over the top of a hill, a deafening screaming noise put us on high alert. My heart was pounding, my mouth dry. Then we saw it. A huge wild elephant.

I cracked it and sprinted off. But Corporal Richardson yelled after me, 'Come back! If he attacks we'll need your 7-62 rifle. My tommy gun bullets'll bounce off him.'

Luckily the elephant continued on his way and we on ours. Welcome to the jungle, I mused. Coming on dark on the second day, we finally found the camp. By now, after two days bumbling through the humid jungle in full gear, lugging pack and rifle, I was knackered.

We had to get our tents ready before darkness fell. I noticed everybody was staking bamboo poles into the ground at an angle, lashing them together to form a framework. A sheet of canvas was hung off this like a hammock. I asked someone why.

'You can't sleep on the ground. Scorpions…' came the casual reply. 'And always check each morning for scorpions – your boots, clothes and equipment,' my helpful comrade continued. 'One more thing,' he added. 'Make sure you put up the mosquito net they issued you over your swag.'

In the jungle we raised our beds off the ground to avoid scorpions and bull ants

The reality of jungle patrols was dawning on me. What had made me sign up for this kind of life?

A local scorpion captured on patrol in the jungle

But my spirits lifted enormously when I overheard Corporal Richardson's laconic comment to my peers: 'Though he's skinny and light, he's a fighter. Doesn't give up.'

Whilst on jungle patrols, we survived on ration packs. Each and every pack included boiled rice. The monotony of the diet put me off boiled rice for life. In my later civilian life, whenever faced with rice on a menu, I could only stomach fried rice.

Jungle Patrols 35

*

The next few weeks we spent scouring the jungle for insurgents. We regularly moved camp. Some days we spent patrolling local areas – mainly the Thai–Malay border as well as villages and towns such as Ipoh, a major tin-producing area. The locals always greeted us warmly. I guess they preferred us over the communists.

On patrol, we often had to wade through rivers and creeks. Therein lay a problem – blood-sucking leeches. Awful things. Once you were clear of the water, you had to down packs and rid your legs of the leeches. They could not be pulled off – but if I lit a cigarette I could burn them off. Waste of a cigarette. Worse, there might be three or four water-crossings a day requiring a leech burn-off. I hated it.

Nightguard duty was particularly scary for those of us not used to the bush. Each man in the platoon was assigned a couple of hours every second night. This meant patrolling the camp perimeter in the pitch black. No torchlight was allowed, so we groped and stumbled, trying not to be heard, trying not to fall. A story began circulating of a Kiwi soldier on night duty who had supposedly been dragged from camp by a tiger, mauled and killed.

So every time I was on duty I would feel my way forward with hands and feet, alert to stumps, creepers, thorny bush, trying to avoid the tangle of vines that hung from the tree canopy above. One particular night I was completely petrified, convinced that either a tiger or enemy combatant was following me around the perimeter. To this day, I still believe something was out there.

*

Jungle patrols lasted a couple of months. Given my platoon had been out for a while, we were soon heading back to Camp Terendak, but not before a sergeant we nicknamed Tiny – a huge 23-stone bloke – broke his leg. It was impossible terrain for a helicopter to land and retrieve him, so we had to carry him out on a makeshift stretcher. We carried him, four men at a time – in shifts – everybody taking a turn. I was just nine stone, so it was tough. The terrain was mountainous and difficult, so we were forced to stop constantly to catch our breath. But with Tiny in agony, none of us felt we could rest for long. The quicker we got him down the mountain, the better. This medevac through the jungle was probably the toughest of my Malaya experiences. By the time we reached Camp Terendak three days later, everybody was exhausted. Fortunately we were given time to rest and recover.

Our jungle assignments were mostly limited to one principal area. Here we would routinely set up a new base camp from which to patrol. Being constantly on the move, cleaning weapons, setting up camp, and confined to our darkened tents after night fell, time passed quickly.

Out on patrol, I was made forward scout – meaning if we got lost I was to blame. This role also made me 'first responder' – whether to animal or human encounters. On one occasion, leading the platoon, as I skirted around a huge bush, I looked up to find a huge tiger staring me in the face. Both tiger and I fled – in opposite directions.

Thankfully the tiger kept its distance. But despite my love for these wild beasts, my nerves were shattered – I could not stop shaking. I reasoned that the tiger, mysteriously aware I was a Balmain Tigers fan, had spared me in a sense of brotherhood.

*

Some time later, as I traipsed along a jungle path, I jumped over a log. As I did so, the thing moved. It was a huge python and I ran like a world record holder. I had heard that Malayan pythons loved to kill goats or small cattle by suffocating them, before swallowing them whole. As the snake slithered away, the boys – well back behind – yelled at me to come back. Thank God we had no enemy combatants to deal with on that patrol.

Pythons such as this could kill and digest a calf

Jungle assignments lasted sometimes weeks and occasionally for months. Patrolling was tough at times, not just because of the snakes and tigers. We also had to contend with searing humidity, mosquitoes and scorpions. Even though we took ghastly anti-malarials, a few of us still came down with malaria.

Given the mountainous terrain and the fact that we were on the move all the time, forced marches lugging all our gear required stamina. Patrolling from a base camp was a little easier, as we only carried our weapons and small amounts of food and water.

While I wondered how I would react under fire, I never wanted to find out. On one occasion we were patrolling the Malaya–Thai border – with live rounds loaded. On a jungle track, our mission was to locate a particular elevated cave which had a sightline over the valley. From there, we would be more easily be able to sight communist insurgents.

But to access the cave we had to traverse a tight corner heavily forested with dense bamboo. Our head scout rounded this corner, disappearing into the greenery. His orders were to unload his weapon before entering the cave.

Suddenly we heard the boom of gunfire. Had our scout been ambushed? The rest of our platoon all froze in terror, uncertain what to do.

We were sheepish when we learned there was no enemy (I would not be telling this story otherwise). Our head scout had simply discharged his own rifle accidently.

Our food and weapon replenishments were ferried on Borneo pack ponies handled by a mixture of Aussies, Kiwis and Koylies. They delivered supplies into different areas daily. The ponies reminded me of the strong little buggers which the ANZACs had relied on during the First World War. They could bear a lot of weight. These troops – we called them campwallers – handling the ponies were on a good wicket, able to work out of base camp with full facilities out of harm's way.

Malacca streetscene during my visits

At the time I smoked not only cigarettes but a pipe. That, together with the camouflage of my Army hat, made me appear older than my twenty years. I was also opinionated. So my peers nicknamed me Pop. The moniker stuck and many of the young or immature privates would come to me for advice.

I did my best with these eighteen year olds, though I'm not sure my advice helped. Maybe I helped someone in a small way.

To this day, if I run into an Army mate, they still call me Pop. Even my three grandchildren call me Pop Johnnie. Except for my parents, no one called me John or Johnnie until I was much older. Later, as a civilian, my nickname was 'Skinny'.

Camp Terendak

Finally our platoon settled into some sort of routine in camp – cleaning equipment, eating well, going to town for a few drinks (even though we had a bar in camp). In Camp Terendak we were regularly required to take part in military parades – essentially ceremonial troop formations – characterised by close-order drills and marching. These were often on significant national or military occasions. A display of military precision and tradition, they were designed to showcase our discipline – in fact, the Malayan parades were usually bigger than those held in Australia. Often a local sultan or dignitary was guest of honour. Local families attended, lining the streets clapping like groupies. We always left the parade ground feeling a million dollars.

Our A Company on parade, carrying L1A1 Self loading rifles

1 Platoon, kitted out with packs in readiness for jungle deployment

Trooping the Colour, Camp Terendak

We cleaned our own weapons religiously, but for cleaning of our gear – boots and belts, for instance – the Malay 'Amahs' brought the gear up to a far better standard than we could achieve, for a small outlay. Amahs were very poor, but lovely, friendly people. By engaging their services I felt we were helping them. Amahs also offered a washing and ironing service in camp. Our uniforms always returned in perfect condition – again at a low cost.

The Sultan of Malacca inspecting our Battalion on parade

Me with Chris at Camp Terendak

The city closest to Camp Terendak – Malacca – had a rich history. Founded in the early 15th century, Malacca was famous for its strategic location and rich cultural heritage. It was founded by Paramesva, a

Hindu prince from Sumatra who fled from the Javanese kingdom of Majaphit. He established a small village that grew into a thriving port city due its strategic location, along the Strait of Malacca which became a vital trade route connecting the east to the west. Today the Strait of Malacca is one of the major shipping lanes in the world. The city became a centre for international trade attracting merchants from Arabia, India and China. It was during this time the Malacca Sultanate was established, marking the beginning of Malay political power in the region.

The prosperity of Malacca attracted the attention of European powers. In 1511, the city was conquered by the Portuguese, led by Alfonso de Albuquerque, marking the beginning of a long period of colonial rule. The Portuguese fortified the city and used it as a base for their spice trade which was highly lucrative at the time. However, in 1641, the Dutch seized control from the Portuguese, and Malacca remained under Dutch rule for over a century.

In 1795, during the Napoleonic Wars, the British took control of Malacca to prevent it from falling into French hands. The city was officially ceded to the British in 1824 under the Anglo–Dutch Treaty, and it became part of the Straits Settlements along with Penang and Singapore. British Malacca's history is mixed up in Malay, Chinese, Indian, Portuguese and Dutch cultures and this multicultural heritage is reflected in the city's architecture, food and traditions.

I found Malacca's history a fascinating tapestry of trade, culture, and colonial influence. The Portuguese influence was obvious in the city's architecture. I was intrigued to see how the locals lived in Kampongs – indigenous villages where whole families lived together in close communities. Given we were so close to Malacca, the enterprising locals appeared everywhere outside the camp and en route to the city. Once we were in Malacca proper, every local seemed to be a taxi driver.

Myself, Ken and mates in a Malacca bar

For me, a huge plus of army life was the key role of sport, given I had a passion for cricket and AFL football. Here in camp, I became involved in any sport on offer, including AFL, soccer, rugby union and volleyball. Our volleyball team practiced every day in our own time – indeed, we knew we were pretty good. We set up our volleyball court on a small parade ground outside our platoon HQ. I was proud when, after some great matches against rival platoons, ours was awarded the champion volleyball team in the entire battalion.

1 Platoon volleyball championship at Camp Terendak (me second from L)

Our Company starting a cross-country course

I made selection in the battalion teams for AFL, soccer and rugby union, competing against England and New Zealand. In those days, Kiwi men were conscripted into their army as a part of national service. So, given their pool of talent – All-Blacks included – competing against New Zealand in rugby union was particularly tough. I remember our first game against the Kiwis. I was horrified to find my skinny self lined up against two huge All-Black centres.

Though it was great fun, I don't know how I survived that first match. I remember being proud as punch when I scored a couple of tries (I dont know how). In November 1962, I sprained by finger on the football field. A year later I sprained my ankle, giving me five days on sedentary duties. But I suffered nothing more serious than that.

Mess hall beers (L Barry Benson, Beetle, Ken McLeod. R Barry Adams & me)

For New Zealanders in the 1960s, the cost of motor vehicles was really high. Moreover, you had to go on a long waiting list. So a lot of New Zealand conscripts used to save up and, just before returning home, would purchase a car in Malaya and ship it to New Zealand – a much cheaper and quicker route to having your own vehicle.

*

Camp life was peaceful for a while. But one day all hell broke loose when a bunch of Koylies bashed up a Kiwi and he died. The New Zealand diggers were furious. Their entire battalion marched on the Koylies camp, ready to tear them to pieces. Finally – with the Military Police stepping in – sanity prevailed and a bloodbath was avoided. But the tensions lingered – the Kiwis never forgave their British allies.

I got on well with the Kiwis, whether they were Māori or whites. At least half of the Kiwi soldiers were Māori and they integrated seamlessly with the Kiwis of Caucasian background. For some reason the Kiwis 'adopted' me as their own. The friendship was like a mafia brotherhood – hurt me, you hurt the whole family. There are consequences.

If we were out on the town and anyone threatened me, they would pipe up, 'Leave our bro alone!' Given the size of my Māori mates, aggressors listened.

There was one bar just outside camp where the brotherhood had its own little corner. No one was allowed to trespass. We used to go across to the Kiwi camp to have a drink sometimes, which meant traversing large stormwater drains, built to handle the tropical storms. One night Barry Adams (a country boy from Albury who we called Chico) and I were staggering home from the Kiwi camp in a drunken stupor. Back at our barracks, I vaguely realised I'd lost Barry.

Not until the next morning did we locate him sleeping in the stormwater drain some way back. Lucky there had been no tropical storm that night as Barry would have been a goner.

Forever after, with a twinkle in his eye, Barry would accuse me of pushing him in and leaving him to die.

When we returned to Camp Terendak after a while in the jungle, routine normalised with regular meals, sport, drinking, and parade exercises. Here we were required only to wear boots, shorts and a cap – a khaki shirt was optional, mandatory only for meals in the mess. Out in the jungle, we also spent plenty of time shirtless. We had never even heard of protective sunscreen. In an age before any awareness of skin cancer, my fair skin was attacked by the tropical sun daily[3].

Christmas Eve drinks 1962 at the mess hall, Camp Terendak (LtoR): Bing Crosby; ?,?,? Me (standing); Dutchy Holland; Barry Adams; ?, Ken McLeod

---

3 As I aged, basal and squamous cell carcinomas appeared on my forearms, scalp, legs, upper back, forehead, cheeks and ears with persistent regularity. Countless visits to a skin cancer specialist ensued, treating scores of lesions. In the last eleven years alone, twenty have been burned off or surgically excised.

Hollywood, Recreation & Federation

In 1963, international stars descended on our small camp when Hollywood actor William Holden, French fashion model and actress Capucine, and Japanese leading man Tetsurō Tamba arrived to film an adaptation of the 1960 novel *The Durian Tree* about the communist uprising in Malaya. The story was set in 1953 as the Malayan communist insurgency erupted while Britain was preparing to grant Malaya independence.

By now Holden (his real surname was Beedle) was 45 and had been a Hollywood sensation for well over two decades. At the time, his most widely recognised and most successful role had been in David Lean's 1957 *The Bridge on the River Kwai* with Alec Guinness. Holden also had been best man and one of only two guests at Ronald and Nancy Reagan's 1952 wedding. Capucine – ten years younger – was the stage name of Germaine Lefebvre[4].

The drama *The 7th Dawn*[5] (at one stage titled *The Third Road* and *Ten Days to Penang*) was to be released in newfangled Technicolor. But the director, Lewis Gilbert, needed some soldiers as extras. Holden was impressed with we Aussies doing cartwheels and tumbling about in rivers and lakes. The director, too, admitted we were pretty tough. If they relied on stuntmen, he would need to supply mattress foam to soften their falls, not to mention pay them a fortune. In comparison, we were free labour. I was one of those chosen. Given I was a movie buff and had even worked in the business, I was thrilled to be involved in shooting scenes.

The film location was some way from Camp Terendak and it was the monsoon season, so it rained daily. Both stars and crew used to have a betting competition – for good money – in predicting the time the downpour would start each day. When William Holden won, he would put his winnings on the bar for we Aussie soldiers.

For those weeks of filming, we had a ball. Little army discipline, good food, plenty of beer, and lots of laughs. The script included a nude scene for Susannah York, who was not keen to do it, but the filmmakers insisted. She appeared in one take and her stand-in appeared in another. Photos of York shooting the scene were later published in *Playboy* magazine.

After its release, *Variety* magazine wrote: 'Despite script deficiencies and some static direction, [the film] has sufficient action-adventure elements to make it a reasonable box office contender, with William Holden's name as lure.' In fact, the film was not a hit, not even recouping its costs, though definitely worth watching.

---

4 Holden and Cappucin reportedly began a two-year affair, which ended due to Holden's alcoholism.
5 Serendipitously, the woman I would later marry was also Dawn.

Film stars in Malaya for the shooting of The 7th Dawn (LtoR William Holden director Lewis Gilbert; Capucine; Tetsuro Tamba)

We privates in extras roles during filming with a local kampong as backdrop

Myself wading through a swamp in a scene from The 7th Dawn

Actors and director Lewis Gilbert take a break on the 7th Dawn set.

A sizable crew supported the action behind the scenes

*

My next adventure was a military training exercise which involved climbing out of a helicopter carrying full gear and weapons. When the chopper was 40 to 50 feet above the ground, it hovered and a thick rope thrown out for us to climb down.

As I waited for my turn, I watched as the soldier in front of me grappled with the rope. Suddenly he lost control and fell. I winced at the angle he hit the ground. All I could see was a never-ending rope to descend, with a soldier writhing at the bottom in agony – likely a broken leg (it was). I went numb. Nonetheless, despite a few slips, to my huge relief I made it without falling.

*

One army exercise involved climbing down a rope from a hovering helicopter

The army had set up a recreation camp called Port Stephenson, alongside the Strait of Malacca. Here troops could spend a few days of their downtime or weekend leave. Large tents had been installed with sleeping quarters. For recreation we could use the mess hall and canteen, swim at a nearby beach and fish (unsuccessfully). At night we would drink, play cards, and make fun of each other. The place was in between Camp Terendak and Kuala Lumpur, so we would often organise a few taxis into the city.

A weekend picnic at Port Stephenson, our young company major is second from right

Once, some of us travelled the 500 kilometres north by train to Penang state in northwest Malaya. The state comprised mainland Serebang Perais and Penang Island in the Strait of Malacca. A large RAAF base was housed on the mainland at Butterworth and a short ferry ride away was the state capital, George Town, on the 295 square kilometre Penang Island. George Town was a densely populated tourist hotspot – it is now accessible from the mainland via two road bridges.

George Town I remember as a wonderful place to visit with its colonial architecture, national park, tropical rainforests, and vibrant cultures living side by side. Amidst its blend of Malay, Chinese, Indian and European influences, I stared in wonder at Fort Cornwallis, Chinese temples, the Indian-style Kapitan Keling Mosque, and the Buddhist Keylok si Temple.

Some R&R at Camp Stephenson. Malay boys would cook and wash and take our clothes for laundering. Dutchy Holland in the middle

In the heart of the oldest part of George Town, amongst narrow, winding lanes and quaint-looking pre-war houses I came across Khoo Kongsi – a grand Hokkien clanhouse. Its elaborate and highly ornamented architecture reflected the dominant presence of the Chinese in the region. It even housed a traditional theatre and late 19th-century rowhouses for clan members, all clustered around a granite-paved square.

Khoo Kongsi temple in Georgetown

Georgetown street scene 1960s

Georgetown, Penang state 1960s

On 16 September 1963, we were back at Camp Terendak when Malaya, North Borneo (renamed Sabah), Sarawak and Singapore[6] united together as the Federation of Malaysia. Brunei chose to remain a British protectorate (and later became independent as a small, oil-rich Malay sultanate).[7]

On September 16, 1963 this installation in Kuala Lumpur was lit up to mark the formation of the Federation of Malaysia

We were in a Malacca bar celebrating independence with some locals. I recall towards the end of the evening being with a local girl. McKenzie – the notorious drinker – was with us, plastered. At the end of the night this girl and I went to get a taxi – I offered to drop her home then continue to the barracks. But McKenzie decided *he*

---

6 *Given deep political and economic differences between the ruling parties of Singapore and Malaya, Singapore would not last long in the union, separating from Malaysia in August 1965.*
7 *Indonesia was not happy with this union, given the greater power it gave its Muslim neighbour. A breakdown in political, economic and social relations ensued, leading to armed incursions, bomb attacks and other terrorist activities by Indonesian groups. For example, Indonesian troops who parachuted into Malaya were arrested. We Commonwealth troops were careful not to get involved, to avoid the tension escalating.*

wanted this girl and started carrying on. He towered over my slight frame, so there was no way I was getting into a fight with him. Instead we ran down the stairs. Luckily there was a cab outside. We jumped in. However McKenzie lurched close behind, hailing another cab which began chasing us back and forth through the streets of Malacca. My driver handled his cab better, so we finally lost him. In retrospect, it was like a Keystone Cops movie, though I was completely terrified at the time.

I dropped the girl off and returned to camp as soon as I could. The next morning over breakfast in the mess hall, McKenzie grinned amicably. It became clear he had no memory of his great taxi chase. Alcohol-induced memory loss was common for this guy.

Borneo Ponies

The Jungle Warfare School ouside Johor Bahru would be my home for six months

After returning from one jungle patrol, I was startled to hear I was being transferred by army truck to a camp near Johore Bahru, 230 kilometres south-east at the southern tip of Malaya, just across the causeway from Singapore. To add to my cholera prophylactics, I was ordered to have a smallpox vaccination. It was October 1963.

The Jungle Warfare school, as it was known, was a large, easy-going camp housing located in Kota Tinggi, known for training soldiers in jungle combat environments – mostly Malay and Gurkha troops.

This Gurkha British military division had been formed as part of the response to the Malayan Emergency and was known officially as the 17th Gurkha Division/Overseas Commonwealth Land Forces. They used a black cat as their emblem. Gurkhas were highly respected, known for their bravery and skill, with a reputation as reliable and disciplined warriors. I had already heard about their fierce fighting style with a Khukuri – a curved knife.

I found these guys to be lovely people. Each morning as we walked around the camp it was impossible to miss the aroma of breakfast curry emanating from their mess hall. This camp also had a good canteen and movie house. It was like being on holidays. If we did our job no one bothered us.

Our platoon's sleeping quarters at the Jungle Warfare school offered no privacy and little storage space

Playing basketball at the Jungle Warfare base

My new role would be a handler of the military's Borneo ponies. Also known as Kuda Padi, rice horse or paddy horse, Borneo ponies – barely 12 hands high – are native to the states of Kelantan and Trengganu. At the time they were mostly owned by the wealthier class and employed in draft work or riding. In the military we used them as pack ponies to ferry supplies to troops in the bush.

Me on one of my two ponies

Our ponies stables were open to allow ventilation and the floor could easily be hosed down

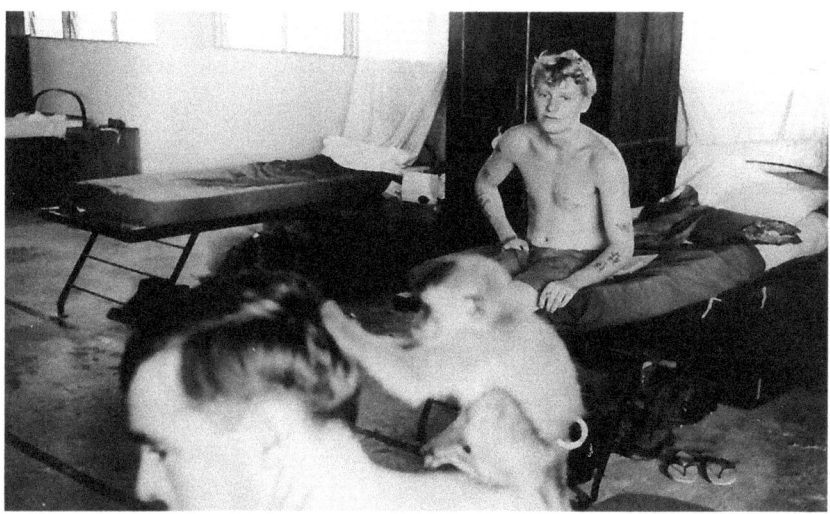

Our two Pommie team members with a popular visitor

I would be one of just two Australians, two New Zealanders, and two Koylies chosen to be a handler. I have no idea who put my name forward but whoever it was, I am eternally grateful. The Pommie sergeant in charge of our team was a really nice fellow, who insisted on treating us as equals. He was not so bothered with the routine army discipline but instead had a passion for horses. He kept a thoroughbred in the stables, which he would ride locally, taking him over our jumps, though I don't recall him ever racing.

Borneo ponies tended to be very quiet animals when carrying supplies in the jungle, but here they could sometimes be crazy. Our daily duties included taking the ponies for a ride in a rubber plantation across the road. I recall we would be jogging along then, without warning, they would take off. Despite their size, it took all my strength to rein them in from a gallop. My hands would be clutched around the pommel, reins all but useless, as my pony charged across a busy thoroughfare, narrowly missing a collision with cars, trucks and carts. We were clearly not trained horsemen.

To keep them fit and exercised, we would ride them over small jumps – though their efforts would never have won a prize. Some days they careered over the obstacles beautifully. But on an off day, my mount would pull up suddenly, just before the jump, sending me flying forward. My body somersaulted over my pony's raised ears, making contact with the ground with a dull thud. I was only thankful these beasts had such short legs that I didn't have far to fall. Their liveliness came through in other ways, too, as they hated being restrained.

Borneo ponies could stop suddenly, throwing us headfirst onto the ground

We regularly exercised our ponies over modest jumps

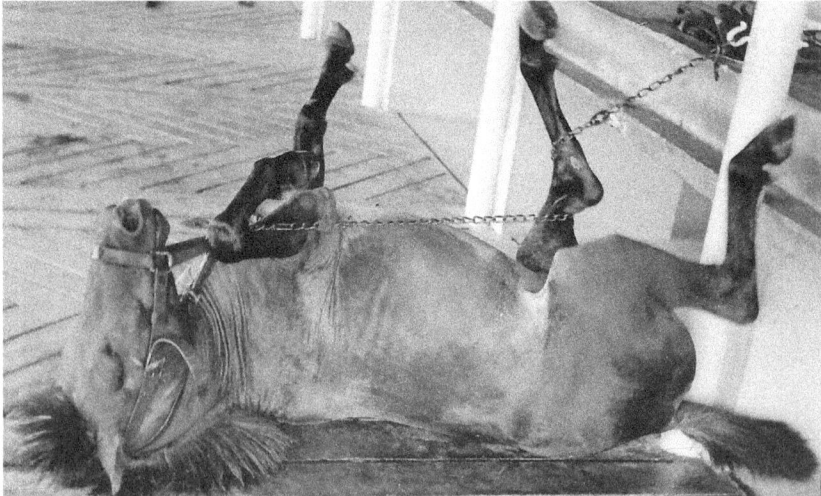

Some of our ponies hated to be chained up at night

Each night one of us would be on duty at the stables. At times there would be a great commotion with the ponies writhing around on the tiled stable floor, entangled in the chains that were supposed to retain them.

All of us pony handlers got on really well and Singapore was a cheap taxi ride away. So on our days off, Singapore was our first port of call, initially at the British Army's Services Club – the Brittania – for cheap booze. This was a two-storey structure with a swimming pool in the forecourt from where we would hit the town's hotspots. It was close to the famous Raffles Hotel, which attracted a very stuck-up 'aristocratic' British crowd. Our rowdy lot were never welcome there. The Brittania was our place.

Singapore's Brittania Club was a refuge for we privates on leave

Singapore, full of servicemen, was cheap. Boogie Street and Chinatown were noisy and raucous – with bars lining the streets, transvestites and servicemen rolling in and out of doss houses. Gonorrhea was a common result, though treatable on base with antibiotics. In the movie houses you could smoke and drink. I recall deep stormwater drains ran through the city to drain away the water from tropical storms. But they were open drains. People would spit in them, go to the toilet in them. A complete contrast to the sedate Singapore of today.

I was impressed to find I could buy beer anywhere. Opium also was very popular with the troops, but not something I tried. But things were changing. Lee Kuan Yew had first been elected Prime Minister in 1959, the country's first under Singapore's new system of self-government. Incredibly, his policies meant he would remain in power until 1990, transforming Singapore from a small wild town into a major city.

The PM's philosophy impressed me: 'A society, to be successful, must maintain a balance between nurturing excellence and encouraging the average to improve.'

As the years progressed, Lee Kuan Yew would introduce strict laws on smoking and spitting in public. You risked a gaol sentence if you broke the new rules. Eventually Singaporeans began to appreciate the benefits and cooperated. I returned to Singapore in the 1990s, 2000s and 2020s and the pristine streets and affluent population never cease to amaze me, given the poverty I witnessed in the 1960s.

Me and fello private Bob Meliere, taken in Singapore

*

Our base camp at the Jungle Warfare school promised comfortable beds every night and a staff canteen. But, of course, it was not all play. The infantry continued to search for insurgents in the Malay jungle. So, from base camp, we pony handlers loaded our ponies up each day and were sent off to the jungle to replenish the troops' supplies, lugging our rifles, walking beside our heavily laden ponies. They were strong little buggers and did not seem to mind the burden. In the jungle, unlike camp, they caused no trouble.

We loaded up our ponies with metal cases carrying ammo supplies for the troops

On our return from our first trip in the jungle with our ponies, having been out of contact with the outside world for five weeks, we took ourselves to the movie theatre. As the Movie Tone newsreel rolled, I sat up straight in my seat as I watched in disbelief the footage of my idol JFK's assassination:

'On November 22 1963, at approximately 12:30 p.m. local time, President John F. Kennedy was shot dead in Dallas, Texas, while riding in a motorcade with his wife, Jacqueline Kennedy, Texas Governor John Connally, and his wife, Nelly Connally.'

This was followed by a piece on four long-haired gits calling themselves The Beatles who had taken the world by storm. I had never heard of them. I would not forget that newsreel.

*

Dropping off supplies in the jungle so regularly kept us busy and meant catching up with our old mates, who ribbed us incessantly about our cushy work.

Once, walking along a jungle track, one of my ponies – aptly named Tiger – lost his footing and slipped off the side of the track, scrabbling frantically to avoid sliding further into a deep ravine. I hung on to Tiger's reins so tightly they cut into my skin.

Panicking and kicking like shit, supplies falling off his back, my pony looked like a goner. But a few of the handlers rushed to my aid, helping me haul him back upright onto the track. We trudged on as if nothing had happened and Tiger, too, fell straight back into his normal rhythm. All I could think about was how lucky it was the animal had escaped breaking a leg or serious injury, given how far we were from medical help. A broken leg would have meant putting him down with my rifle on the spot. I don't think I could have pulled the trigger. My ponies were as close as my mates.

Back in Johore Bahru I celebrated my 21st birthday in January 1964. It was Australia Day so we all went out, starting at the camp bar, then onto the Britannia Club and then another Singapore bar. It was a huge night and I vaguely recall racing in rickshaws down the grimy streets. The next day, we could not stomach taking out our ponies for their daily exercise.

After a few more jungle forays, supplying various Australian, New Zealand and British platoons, more riding at camp, and many more visits to Singapore, our six-month posting was up. We were given orders to return to our respective battalions at Camp Terendak.

On our last night we all made a final visit to Singapore. It was late and a lot of beer had gone down when my Kiwi friends, Tom Tuiwhy and Jerry, turned to me as we walked past a tattoo parlour, their eyes lighting up.

'Let's get tattoos!' they yelled. We designed them on a napkin. One would read: 'Hey you, New Zealand', next to a kangaroo. On the other arm, we would each have inked: 'Who me? Australia', with an image of a Kiwi bird.

'Sure, why not?' I shrugged, trying not to stumble.

I agreed to go first. But by the time the tattooist had seared the agreed designs into each of my forearms, my Kiwi friends had sobered up enough to change their minds. I was somewhat annoyed, though soon forgave the pair and we remained great mates.

On my return home, I regretted the tattoos, wearing long-sleeved shirts to hide them. There was some negative stigma about tatts in those days – mostly sailors and prostitutes had them. I give it little thought today, when, of course, tattoos amongst young Australians are so common.

Anti-Tank Platoon & SEATO

Back at Camp Terendak on 20 August 1963, a year into my posting, I learned my transfer was to 3 RAR battalion. I was assigned to their anti-tank platoon, though I had never noticed tanks in my time in Malaya. Our anti-tank guns were large and heavy, so needed to be towed into position by army jeeps. To adapt to this new role simply required a little practice firing shells a few hundred metres on the artillery range. This also turned out to be another dream posting, involving riding around in vehicles dragging anti-tank artillery behind us. There was little need to venture into the jungle, given artillery was fired from a long distance. On the occasions we did go bush, it was always on roads suitable for rear-echelon personnel – officers and supply teams from HQ.

Our 14 strong anti-tank platoon (me at front left, our Major on far right)

Blocking our ears as we tested our Anti-tank artillery

The officer and sergeant in charge were two of the nicest guys you would ever meet, as were all eight of the soldiers I worked with. Our superiors were like mates, giving we privates no problems. We all blended in well together. Nonetheless, when on the range you had to be on your toes, given the artillery shells were heavy and dangerous. If you mucked up the drills and procedures, you risked doing a lot of damage.

Weekend forays into Malacca continued – on one such adventure, I was slapped with an offence for neglecting to obey. My company commander, Mat Leary, fined me three pounds.

A Company drinks LtoR Don, Ben, me, CSM Frazer (Tiny)

Though we were cocooned from the grunt soldiers, we could not avoid normal army expectations in regard to care of weapons, guard duty, and spotless uniforms. Mind you, given the enormous enclosed camp housed three battalions alongside married quarters, performing guard duty at Camp Terendak was something of a breeze. There was little chance of residents causing trouble. Some mates and I took eight days leave over the Christmas period that year. What with weekends and public holidays, we had a good two weeks to ourselves.

In April 1964, I accepted the Army's offer of an all-expenses paid religious instruction course in Singapore. Like my mates, I couldn't care less about the religious stuff, but the course offered the carrot of five nights' recreation in one of Asia's (then) wildest cities. Many servicemen were based there, and the place was crazy. On the streets it was the Yanks, as usual, who were the silliest. After a few cheap beers at the Brittania, a few tried jumping into the pool from the first-floor balcony. The well-watered crowd cheered them on. That was until one drunk Yank landed on the tiled perimeter instead of the pool. I think we prayed for him the following day at the Church House course. He needed a lot of prayers.

Our spiritual development class in Singapore, April 1964, chaplain 3rd from right

Many of my mates, including Barry, Ken and Cisco, were increasingly pissed off that I was constantly assigned these cushy postings. Barry, in particular, was unhappy, given he had been designated as a signal operator, requiring him to lug around large, heavy wireless operating machinery. Even in the bush he had to carry his wireless as well as his normal gear. In contrast, here's me walking a pony around or sitting in a jeep. It gave us many laughs.

*

A later adventure involved our A Company being dispatched via military aircraft to a regional area of Thailand for several weeks for a SEATO military exercise. The South East Asia Treaty Organisation was then a major contributor to defence capabilities, with eight member countries – Thailand, France, Pakistan, the Philippines, America, Australia, New Zealand and Britain (which had administered Hong Kong, North Borneo and Sarawak)[8]. Founded in 1955, the UK and France had joined partly due to having long-maintained colonies in the region, and partly due to concerns over developments in Indochina. The US, perceiving Southeast Asia as a pivotal frontier for Cold War geopolitics, saw SEATO as essential to its Cold War containment policy.

For this exercise, each nation provided troops, though given we were in Thailand, their troops made up the lion's share. The Thais seemed to have a fetish for colourful uniforms decorated with gold braid. I found them the nicest, gentlest people you could meet. Our anti-tank platoon capabilities had no role, given we could hardly fire massive shells into friendly troops. So for these exercises we returned to our regular infantry functions.

---

8   *Primarily created to block further communist gains in Southeast Asia, SEATO is generally considered a failure. Although SEATO military forces held joint military training, they were never deployed because of internal disagreements. It was dissolved on 30 June 1977, after many of its members lost interest and withdrew.*

Lining up outside our sleeping quarters - the sports stadium - during the SEATO exercise

Market stalls popped up next to the stadium to take advantage on the hundreds of troops with an allowance to spend

M62 drills during the SEATO exercise

Napalm bombs being detonated at a safe distance

We were stationed outside a major town and were given bedding in the sports stadium. I was amazed to see dozens of beer houses and shops pop up out of nowhere, determined to cash in on the multitudes of visiting defence troops. Asians were poor but immensely adaptable. This was too good an opportunity to miss.

The SEATO exercise, held in a valley which had the feeling of an amphitheatre, was quite spectacular. During the war games, visitors could sit back and watch planes flying back and forth, simulated bombing and strafing, even exploding napalm bombs in the distance. This show of strength was like watching a war movie.

With the Yanks we engaged in a simulated jungle exercise, where we were supposed to quiet as ghosts. The Yanks were an utter failure at this, chiaking and crashing through the bush. Thankfully there were no insurgents around. In contrast, they could not believe how quiet we, along with the Kiwis and British, were. We had learnt to use hand signals instead of talking to each other.

The SEATO joint exercises were in the daytime, but our nights were free. Mixing with so many nationalities – especially the Yanks – was an experience. We had come across a few in Singapore, but here in greater numbers their loud brashness, racism, and propensity for pot made them stand out as a different species. White and coloured American servicemen did not get on – many carried knives, and fights between them were not uncommon. In contrast, to the Yanks' bemusement, we Aussies and Kiwis socialised with servicemen whatever their skin colour.

The camp officers had laid down a midnight curfew. However we Aussies and Kiwis were known to go out and drink. On one occasion we were having too good a time in this makeshift town.

What with the drinking, bar girls and food, time slipped away. When we finally called it a night, it was very late. A couple of the Kiwi boys had exited home a little earlier.

As we approached base camp we spied a duty officer waiting outside to book us. Our Kiwi mates had clearly already been busted. So we changed direction, creeping around the back straight to our beds.

For the rest of the posting, the Kiwi boys were grounded, with no pass-outs permitted, while the rest of us continued going out carousing. There was a lot of banter between us about the injustice, but there was a funny side to it.

For the SEATO exercise, the King of Thailand was to visit. Unfortunately a few mates and I were designated guards of honour. The night prior we had been on the booze late, and next morning, lined up as welcome guard, the King's huge helicopter blades above us stirred up a mini tornado. None too steady on our feet, the pilot descended too close. Dust rose from the parade ground in a brown fog and we were blown about like sapling branches. Our slouch hats askew, we managed a very average guard of honour.

Guard of honor to welcome the King of Thailand

The Thai King inspects SEATO troops, his Chinook transport in the background

On his inspection the King had a bit of a laugh, but the occasion was being filmed. When, days later, the high command in Canberra watched the charade via the film footage, they were not happy.

Unfairly, the footage showed the helicopter and our Welcome Guard in separate shots, so it was impossible to see how the helicopter's turbulence had caused such havoc. The officer in charge was landed in more trouble than we were. I felt sorry for our officer, but we just had a good laugh.

We left Thailand, returning to the routine of parades, range practice, and sport at Camp Terendak. My time in Malaya was coming to an end. Australia only had three battalions at that stage. In my two years there, I had served a year each in battalions 2 and 3. I was fortunate to experience so many different facets of infantry life in such a short time – rifleman, forward scout, horse handler, and anti-tank weaponry – few were so lucky. Although the jungle postings had been tough, having officers and NCOs who became more like friends than superiors made a huge difference.

These two years remain the most memorable and rich of my life experiences, exposing me as it did to different cities, cultures, environments and people in one of the great cultural melting pots of the world[9].

---

9 *Camp Terendak would be handed over to the Malaysian army on 28 March 1970 and has been occupied by the 1st Infantry Brigade ever since.*

Back in Sydney

I was being transferred to 1 Battalion at Sydney's Holdsworthy base. Serving in three battalions over such a short period was rare. On return to Sydney, I was offered a promotion, but despite the great experiences, I knew the military was not a long-term career for me.

So I told my superiors they would be better to offer the inducement of promotion to those intent on making a career in Defence.

On 12 August 1964, after a few days off to catch up with family and friends, I reported for duty at 1 Battalion in Holdsworthy. We Sydneysiders were given the choice of commuting from home (except when on night guard duty) or living at the barracks, and I did both at various times. By now my folks had moved nine blocks east to a slightly bigger cottage at 137 Young Street.

My family had moved to this semi at 137 Young St, by the time I returned to Sydney

I settled into a routine of barracks duties and socialising with my Malaya mates who had returned – in particular Barry Adams and Ken Mcleod – now the closest of friends. We would go out in the city most weekends, often to the Civic Hotel on the corner of Pitt and Liverpool Streets, opposite Chequers Night Club. The Civic was known as an army pub. Given we knew it attracted the ladies, we wore our uniforms.

One night Barry, some other mates and I decided to go to the Coogee Bay Hotel in uniform, where the Delltones were performing. The venue was virtually sold out, so when a group of girls arrived, the only seats left were at our table. Having just won their squash tournament, they were out for a big night. But they were not happy to be seated with soldiers. One of them told the staff to please let them know when other seats became available. These young ladies had airs.

But as the night warmed up, we started to talk to each other, finding a lot in common. One of them was Elizabeth, and I took a liking to her. We all adjourned together to Kings Cross for coffee.

However when Barry confessed to me that this Elizabeth was the girl of *his* dreams, I nobly stood aside. A week later, Barry rang her home. He would ultimately marry her a few years later after he returned from Vietnam.

At home after my return from duty in Malaya

At Holdsworthy we were left alone in regard to our army work, though it was humdrum compared to Malaya. There were frequent exercises in the bush around Singleton and Bulli. I was constantly being pressured to stay on past the three years I had signed on for. But an exercise in the Australian bush reinforced my decision to leave when my time was up.

We were out camping on army bivouac for a few weeks. Our commanders loved to make us toil up steep hills – to build our stamina and strength, I guess. On return to camp we were all dirty and exhausted, keen for some leave and relaxation. But instead I was immediately assigned weekend duties while the guys who had remained in camp were given leave. This lack of fairness made my mind up. In civilian life I could at least make my own decisions about my weekends and, indeed, the nature of the work I did.

So for the remainder of my army time, I just breezed along, doing only what I had to, trying not to step out of line.

One of my assignments was guard duty at Victoria Barracks in Paddington. It was not hard work, but watching the inner city public out enjoying themselves every evening was frustrating, especially the drunks making smart comments. On guard duty we had no right of reply.

My formal discharge was approved in November 1964 and finalised the next January. Just prior, our battalion was informed they would be the first full Australian battalion posted to Vietnam. (Most of us did not even know where Vietnam was.) Again, we were informed the fighting would be against communists insurgents. For those who went, it would turn out to be a vicious, dirty, horrific tour.

My mates Barry and Ken stayed on and were posted there. Barry would die of a brain tumour – believed to be caused by exposure to

Agent Orange (though the Army would never admit culpability). On his return, Ken was plagued with what is now known as post-traumatic stress disorder – suffering nightmares and sleep problems. He has survived on a service pension since leaving. They were just two of thousands to suffer physical or mental damage as a result of a conflict which achieved nothing.

For me, returning to civilian life involved a transition in both mind and body. I was sad to farewell my mates but the change was easier as I had made my mind up years earlier and I left on my own terms. Mentally, the transition was much easier than those who left after a decade or more. A friend at the time advised me: 'If you succeed in the army, you can be successful anywhere. Back yourself!'

But what to do next? With only average school results (remember I left after the Intermediate) and limited civilian employment prior to army life, my future felt like the edge of a cliff. But I decided to take the skills the army had given me – leadership, team work, decision making, common sense, discipline, and the ability to problem solve in difficult situations – and use them to contribute to society as a civilian. Crucially, I now also had a wider life experience – an understanding of other cultures.

It was the maturity and confidence I had first nurtured in the army that would see me succeed in a range of managerial positions – in administration, distribution and sales. I ultimately had the confidence to adapt my skills to various industries – photographic, hardware, flooring and logistics.

Dad was one of those cold fellows. I think he loved his family, but growing up he never showed it. But as he got older, he looked out for me more. Perhaps he changed. Observing him at work, he treated people well – all the ladies loved him. Why had he treated Mum and us kids so differently?

I moved out of home, into a share apartment in Glebe. Given he had warehousing industry connections, my father clinched me a warehouse job as a stock records clerk in the electrical firm Phillips Industries. I was starting back at the bottom, but it was something.

In 1969 I took up an accounting role with Watson Victor, a medical supplies company in North Ryde. I remember one fellow, Keith Simmons, was resigning to take up a role with Zenith Hardware. There was a staff farewell at a local pub and a girl called Dawn was there.

Shirley Bassey was due to perform at a venue called Chequers in about two weeks' time. I was desperate to impress in those days, so I took a risk. As I was dropping Dawn home, I promised that if I my tax refund came through, I'll take her to see Bassey (I'd spend money like it was water if I had it).

The refund came through, so that concert was our first real date. By 1971 Dawn Tucker and I were married. We moved into an apartment in West Ryde. Years later we would take advantage of a subsidised Department of Veteran Affairs loan to buy a house in North Rocks.

In 1970 I joined Cutler Hammer as an assistant accountant. My boss was a guy studying accountancy at university. His reconciliations were about 40 pages long, whereas when I did them, they fitted on a page. I couldn't convince him all his extra workings were not needed. I realised, if he's at university, as dumb as he is, I must be able to make something out of my life. It was a real turning point. I realised I had more commonsense and life experience than he would ever have.

Initially based in Camperdown, the Cutler Hammer business eventually relocated to Lane Cove. I remained some years given I had good work mates. We would drink at Balmain Leagues Club every Monday. Meanwhile, to give the local primary kids an outlet for AFL, a group of us founded Annandale Juniors Club. Here I found real joy in coaching junior boys teams for some years. Most of the kids were from poor families without a car. If there was a car, their dad was not usually interested in watching the games. So instead I would cram most of the team into my Vauxhall to ferry them to our away matches in Ermington and North Ryde.

By December 1972, I was ready for a challenge and landed a role as administration manager of warehousing functions with the multinational German/Belgium-owned AGFA Gaevert – who then specialised in photographic film and camera equipment. My role was looking after service departments, logistics and distribution for the NSW territory.

I was never motivated at school, but here I *wanted* to learn, to challenge things. I would constantly come up with new ideas to improve efficiency. Constantly questioning, I believed in innovating. I liked to think about what we should be doing and where we should be heading as a business. We used to have an administration conference every year. At each one I'd walk in the door and my boss would say, 'What surprise have you for us this year, John?'

AGFA's Australian head office – located in Melbourne – was really supportive. They gave me so much opportunity to trial different things. The barrier was my state manager. He held me back, knowing my innovations threatened his own job.

My state manager at AGFA, John Schrauwen, was very sales-orientated but he did not understand human resources. He was inefficient in his time management. Regularly his sales staff would be kept back for hours after 5pm for meetings because he had not found time to schedule them during working hours. It was depriving staff of time with their families. That unfairness used to frustrate me.

Other frustrations built up. There was one warehouse employee – a very good friend of mine – who twice refused to do tasks assigned him. There was no option but to sack him. My manager agreed, but when I did fire him, he kept fretting – What if this happens? What if that happens? He went on and on with his concerns every day.

As a personality, Schrauwen was a nice bloke who had some rapport with senior management. They knew his performance was very average but were reluctant to get rid of him given he'd been there so long. When I finally gave my notice in late 1985 after 13 years, senior management flew up from Melbourne, begging me not to leave. I was assured the state manager role was mine if I just waited.

I could not wait. Instead, I took a role with Mitre 10 as their NSW distribution manager. In fact they owned a distribution company – Simco – which imported many of their products from Asian markets to sell in the Mitre 10 stores. I managed Simco and its warehouse functions.

We had a team of buyers who had to talk to me about the latest products with a mind to what the stores needed. I had to work out whether and where their proposed line items would fit – in the warehouse and in the stores. There might be decisions about ousting a poor-selling line to fit in something new.

At Mitre 10 the cooperative structure of the business would cause ongoing problems. Each director was a store owner, and each was a part-owner of the Mitre 10 cooperative and so had some decision-making power. Some supported new ideas or products, others were far more worried about implications for their particular store. Would a proposed new line sell in their area? Each of dozens of store owners would want a say. It meant working for too many bosses.

Our head office boss had an expectation that, whether on work or free time, if we were passing through a town with a Mitre 10 store, we would make a courtesy call to strengthen 'member' relationships. I recall we were all up north in Port Macquarie at a three-day work conference with Mitre 10 store owners.

Driving home to Sydney, given we had just been with the member store owners at the company conference, a few of us instead visited friends en route. When our boss Paul Waite found out, we were yelled at and humiliated. That's how he was. Mitre 10 members were king.

By early 1988, Mitre 10's management team wanted to see what we could learn from the rest of the world. I was asked to accompany Paul Waite on an international fact-finding mission, visiting hardware distribution centres in the US, Canada, Europe, Denmark and Sweden.

Overseas companies were happy to answer our questions and share information – the Canadians and Yanks, in particular. What we discovered in North America were enormous warehouses which doubled as the consumer salesfloor – a centralised direct-to-customer model, allowing operators to buy in bulk, hence cut costs. Costco and Walmart had pioneered the consumer-facing warehouse model in the early 1980s. I saw with my own eyes how popular it was.

I rubbed my boss up the wrong way several times during our travels over incidents which bruised his ego. So on the flights between cities, instead of small talk, I wrote up my notes so I was prepared for the next site visit. I was clear in my recommendations for Mitre 10 to adopt the direct-to-consumer warehouse model throughout Australia.

Our managing director used my glowing reports to put such a proposal to the board. But given board members were mostly self-interested shop owners keen to protect their own turf, such a model scared them. Would they not lose business? The proposal was voted down. On reflection, our managing director, while believing in the model, was more interested in keeping the peace amongst his board.

I resigned in July 1988, immensely frustrated by the lack of foresight. Of course, not long after, organisations such as Bunnings would make a fortune from the same distribution model.

From Mitre 10, I progressed to a customer service manager role with Zenith, a family-owned international importer and distributor who supplied to the hardware industry. My new boss was a good bloke and I loved the challenges that the role threw up.

Unfortunately within little more than a year, a Melbourne-based company, Ramset Fasteners, acquired Zenith, and decided changes were needed. They brought in their own people, so in September 1989 I was left with a redundancy package. They would go on to adopt my design for their new Smithfield warehouse.

From there I was approached by another family-run business – Bryce and Duncan. They were a flooring accessories provider attached to a major worldwide flooring company. They sold all the elements that lie under a carpet – adhesives, glues, nails and grippers. The business initially had one managing director – an old bloke in Adelaide who was really good. Then they promoted a young accountant from Melbourne as joint managing director. When the old bloke retired, unfortunately around five years into my tenure, the new young director ran the business into the ground. The company ended up in receivership, though to their credit, I was paid all my leave and service entitlements before other creditors.

A year on I took on a role with one of their suppliers – Duraloid – a company which distributed natural cork product used in counter toppings and bulletin boards (supplied by the Europe-based Forbo flooring company). In those days natural products were the bee's knees given they were so environmentally friendly. The product had never been strong in New South Wales, so they asked me to come on as state manager to grow that state's market share. I would be the only Sydney-based employee, which meant I would be working on my own for the first time in my life, running my own show.

We also had a product called Pivotelli – used in pivot brackets to mount televisions to walls. I loved being up against the competition – being able to measure progress by improving our sales figures, our market share, or winning more contracts.

For domestic use, the product really needed to be specified by architects. But I discovered these professionals were too busy. Instead, back then, big architecture firms employed a librarian. Architects would go to them to let them know what products were available and the specifications of each. So I made it my business to get to know every Sydney firm's librarian. I would march around the city, sweet-talking these nice women into advocating for my product.

I was so proud to show the company I could increase annual sales from $100,000 to a million in a matter of one year. Part of this success came through winning a contract to install thousands of these Pivotelli brackets for the Olympic Stadium. I stayed over 20 years with Duraloid.

My last role was with Southern Cross Textiles, on a part-time basis for a decade up until 2022.

Given my origins in the Sydney slums with limited schooling, if it had not been for those three years in Defence, I would never have achieved the career I did. Those years taught me self reliance and discipline – the ability to look after myself, my gear and equipment. I came to understand my limits – remember Private Mackenzie carrying my pack as I struggled to complete a 42 kilometre forced march. They built confidence and resilience - showing me that even in a foreign land I had the capacity and wherewithal to care for not only myself, but my mates and my pack animals.

Exercises in the Malayan jungle exposed me not to the enemy – I never even saw a guerilla insurgent – but to different challenges - scorpions, monkeys, elephants and tigers - far from my comfort zone. Weekend escapades into exotic towns, being chased through the laneways of Malacca, interacting with locals and foreign servicemen alike, started to build in me a belief that yes, there was a place in the world for me to give back and thrive. For that I will be forever grateful.

The Service medals I was awarded years after my time in Malaya

www.ingramcontent.com/pod-product-compliance
Lightning Source LLC
Chambersburg PA
CBHW061210070526
44583CB00025B/3191